The Story of Jesus

AWARD PUBLICATIONS LIMITED

ISBN 978-1-84135-744-7

Copyright © 2009 Award Publications Limited
℗ 2009 Award Publications Limited

Read by Sophie Aldred
Music composed by Tim King

All rights reserved. No part of this publication may be reproduced or utilized in any form or by any means electronic or mechanical, including photocopying, recording, or by any information storage and retrieval system now known or hereafter invented, without the prior written permission of the publisher.

First published 2009

Published by Award Publications Limited,
The Old Riding School, The Welbeck Estate,
Worksop, Nottinghamshire, S80 3LR

www.awardpublications.co.uk

09 1

Printed in China

Once, long ago, a kind young woman called  was at home in Nazareth when an  visited her. The name of the  was Gabriel, and he told the virgin  that God had sent him. "You will have a 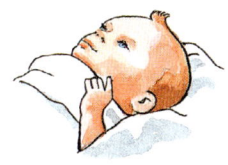," the  said. "He will be the Son of God, and his name will be Jesus."

A man called  lived in the same town as . They were engaged to be married. He worked as a carpenter, and  liked to watch him at work. Even if  was busy making a  or mending a  for a cart, he always had time for .

Soon,  was due to have her 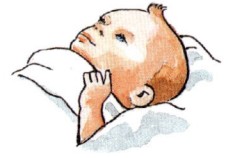. She was very happy.

But poor  was very worried when he heard that the  had commanded that everyone must travel to Bethlehem to be counted.

"We must go," he told .

"I will get some food ready for the journey,"  said. When everything was ready they set out.  rode on a  and walked beside her.

What crowds there were in Bethlehem! It was growing dark when they arrived, and  tried to find a place to stay. He could see how tired  was. But every  and lodging was already full.

Then, at last,  came across a kind-hearted  who offered them his . Gratefully,  accepted.

The   was usually used only for the animals, but the  and the  were calm and sleepy, and did not bother  and  at all.

That night, 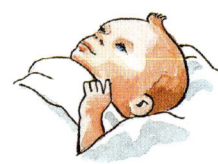 Jesus was born and  wrapped him in swaddling clothes.  filled the  with clean straw so that  could lay him there.

In the morning, some  came to the . When they saw the 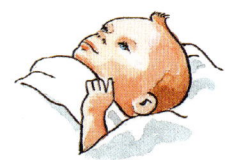 in the , wrapped in swaddling clothes, they were filled with joy. "It is just as the  said," one  whispered. "He is Christ the Lord!"

A bright new  in the east was a sign to three  that a new  had been born.

The  followed the  through many lands until, at last, they found the 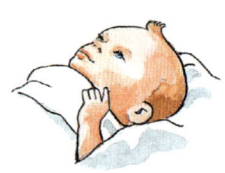 Jesus in Bethlehem. They bowed low before him and offered him the  they had chosen to be fit for a great .

Then, they mounted their  and rode swiftly away, back to their own land.

Leaving Bethlehem,  did not take his little family back to Nazareth.

Instead, he took the 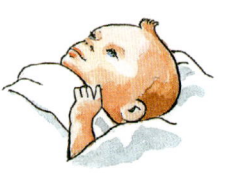 and  to Egypt where they would be safe from the wicked  Herod.

Herod had tried to find the holy child so that he could have him killed. But  had been warned in a dream to leave Bethlehem before

Herod's 🪖 could discover where they lived.

Only when the wicked  died did they go back to live in Nazareth.  grew up in Nazareth. He went to school like the other boys and when he was grown-up he became a carpenter like  . Sometimes,  talked to the  on the shore of Lake Galilee.  told them about the Kingdom

of Heaven as they sat by their

 mending their 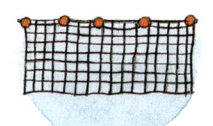 .

Two of the  were brothers.

They wanted to be like  .

"We will follow you," they said.

And so they left their  and their  and they followed him.

One of the  was called Peter. He went everywhere with .

Once, he joined a great crowd of people who had come to hear  speak. The people wanted to stay and listen even when they grew tired and hungry.  took a little boy's

supper of two  and some small

 and divided it up until

there was enough  to feed all

the people. Peter was astonished!

There was even enough  left over to fill twelve  !

Sometimes,  talked about going to heaven. He told Peter and his friends that he would not be with them for long.

The day came when  said he must go to Jerusalem, and his friends found a  for him to ride.

The crowds were so happy to see , they waved  in the air and greeted him with shouts of joy.

But there were some people in Jerusalem who were plotting to kill 🧔 .

That same week, 🪖 came to the quiet little garden where 🧔 was praying. The 🪖 took him away and put him in prison, and soon after, 🧔 was sentenced to die on the ✝ .

The day   died on the

was a sad day for Peter and his friends.

But  did not leave them for long.

He came down from heaven to be with

them again for a short time, filling

their hearts with joy and happiness.